Burning Number Five

Power Plant Poems

Cindy Huyser

Burning Number Five

Power Plant Poems

Cindy Huyser

Blue Horse Press
PO Box 7000 – 148 Redondo Beach, CA 90277
2014

Cover art: Cindy Huyser

Editors: Jeffrey Alfier and Tobi Cogswell

ISBN- 9780692249963

Contents

Acknowledgements iv

Blow-out: 0330 1

The Walk-Down 3

The Properties of Water 5

Gas Yard 6

Transformation 7

Turbine 8

Heat 9

Furnace Leak 11

Burning Number Five 12

Rosebud 13

Night Shift on the Turbine Floor 15

The Dam 16

Until the Outage 18

Turbine Overhaul 20

Lock Out / Tag Out 21

Confined Space Entry 22

Exhalation 23

The Lady in White 24

The Intimacy of Machines 26

Glossary 28

Author's Bio 30

Acknowledgments

"Blow-Out: 0330" first appeared in *Di-Verse-City* (Austin Poets International, Inc., 2005)

"Burning Number Five" first appeared in *San Pedro River Review* (Vol. 6 No. 1, Spring 2014)

"Exhalation" first appeared in *The Enigmatist* (January, 2011)

To my former coworkers
at Holly Street Power Plant

Blow-out: 0330

Some mornings at the plant
are quiet.

03:30, Friday night turned to Saturday,
no machines running,
only routines call.
A hydrogen alarm sounds:
red bottles lined up on a wooden rack,
the four feeding the generator
now empty.

He was four months
from retirement that night
when he caught the tipping cylinder,
then stretched for the block valve—
and old sewing came loose;
he clutched the sudden distension
of his belly
up the elevator
on his way to the emergency room
via the shift supervisor

who'd caught a tipping cylinder
years ago as its shoulder smashed
into another   breaking finger bone
in twenty places

instinct saying better this reaction
than a metal balloon
of hydrogen   let loose
bottle becoming rocket

thoughts of flying cylinder
and sparking steel
exploding the early darkness.

The Walk-Down

I am like a lover
attending the beloved,
a doctor
attending a patient:
every day, wanting to know her,
needing to know
her temperatures, her sounds,
her smells.

From the ninth floor down
to the basement, out
to the gas yard, the lake, I look
at her, and press against her. I gaze
at the levels in each sight glass;
on the preheater floor, draw out and dip
the slender stick that shows
the oil level in the lower bearing.

I peer down into the swirling flame
of her furnace. Her breath beats loud
in my chest as I walk the forced draft fans,
head level with the center
of their great vanes. I meet her
at the shore of the lake, clear
her traveling water screens, follow
her fuel oil lines out to the tanks.

That first hour every day: caressing
her, turning every cuno filter. Blowing down
her accumulated liquids, feeling
her every motor for heat, for vibration.

The Properties of Water

Even a cook in Denver knows
the boiling point of water
changes with pressure,
though not the same way we do:
the Mollier diagram's sleek curves,
the steam tables' neat columns
of numbers.

Water at eighteen hundred
pounds, six hundred degrees,
refracts gray through the port glass
in the camera's eye.

Entropy, enthalpy—even skeptics
are converted on pressure's liberation.
Twin jets of steam erupt
from the water-side stem
as the valve comes off its seat.
We instantly believe, quicken
our gloved and working hands.

Gas Yard

Here are the valves, regulators, knockout tanks
the screaming high pitch of flow
the aching smell
the explosive radio keying area.

Here are the stinking black pits,
the oily liquid we liberate
from the knockout tanks
every shift.

Here is the bypass valve
the careful manual transfer
as furnace flames roar in and out
to the main gas valve's wild oscillation.

Trying to hold the unit on-line,
gas screaming all around.
Trying hard to hear
the radioed instructions.

Transformation

Is the steam dry enough yet?
We have thrown open
the vents and drains,
applied hours of fire
and burner tilt.

Chemical to thermal,
thermal to kinetic—
when we opened the main steam stop valve
too early, slugs of water slammed, swayed
the 20" line inches on its hangers.

We are eager
to latch the turbine, admit steam
to its blading, where a drop of water
behaves as a bullet.
Up on the sixth floor, the vents
have been screaming for some time.
Is the steam dry enough yet?

Mollier diagram, we cling to your curves
as the clock's hands shift,
the pressure inches upward.

Turbine

She smells of hot lube oil,
big body humming with steam,
sucking out its energy
with fixed and moveable blades.

Turbine oil bathes her journal bearings,
she pushes against thrust shoes.
The boiler builds up pressure
and she clamps down.

All day long, latched
in spring-loaded détente,
she throttles fifteen-hundred pound,
thousand-degree steam.

Hours on the turbine floor, drenched in her heat,
both of us driven. She spins up to soak speed,
then on to sync, she enters the marriage
of commutator and slip ring, the sacrament

of impulse and reaction,
steam gland and hood seal.
Her moving blades pass fixed ones
by thousandths of an inch.

Heat

Today, at 95°
next to the machine it's 110°,
though by the vent
it's 120°;

by the leaking valves
on the mezzanine floor
sweat pours down,
sticks pants to legs.
One day, I stepped outside
to 103°
and felt relief.

And up on the boiler—
on the preheater deck—
it's 115°

and all along the 8th floor, 130°
the heat makes it hard to breathe.

Crouching by the secondary
superheater outlet
to close the vent
it's 145°
skin tightens with the searing

though the hot spot
on another unit
is 153°—

remember
to drink water—

I make my way
back
downstairs.

Furnace Leak

Devil's breath
on the 6th floor deck
as the refractory
fails and fails—
at end of the header
my face jerks away,
my hand cannot hold the rail.

Tape it off,
tape it off.

The boiler skin,
a corrugated envelope
rusting with extremity,
weeps a little
after the rain.

Burning Number Five

At seventeen degrees, the oil will spill
as slow as cold molasses. Both back tanks
gauge out at eighteen feet. We climb to fill
the donkey boiler, boots on wobbling planks,
then trudge out to the pump house. Down its stairs
stinks thick, black oil, trapped in symmetric sumps.
We bang valves into place, and back upstairs
purge steam lines free of water. *Start the pumps.*

Inside the furnace, one by one, we slide
each slender metal gun and latch its port.
Two turns of steam, then oil; ignitor's flare.
We peer through cobalt at the brilliant light.
We'll need asbestos gloves to take them out.
My breath blows white into the brittle air.

Rosebud

Six stories up,
on a fan deck slick with ice,
the wind blows hard,
pushes us against railing
as we slip and pick
toward the frozen linkage,
cheaters in hand.

One by one,
transmitters freeze.
All controls to manual
we bump the load control up
then down, up then down,
hoping to move gas valves,
to vary the water.

Already, in Houston,
there are rotating blackouts.

A welder in three pair of overalls
stands between megawatts and off-line,
training his torch on a gland water line,
while an operator releases an oil gun
from its furnace port overhead—
struggling to keep the tip down,
to keep from wearing hot, black fuel.

We drive on banned roads,
work an extra 12 hours after our 12,
wait for relief delivered by
4-wheel-drive vehicles.
We hold these machines on line
while power goes to Dallas,
all of Austin's lights on.
We take turns relieving the welder
outside, holding the rosebud.

Night Shift on the Turbine Floor

After Charles Wright's "Clear Night"

Night shift, turbine floor, dangling incandescent bulbs.
Steam courses through throttle valves, governor,
    and blading.
Black-rimmed gauges shake. The floating foundation
trembles through my boots to its own settling
    frequency.

I long to be one with this machine: steam-driven,
    spinning, and shifting.
I long to feel my bearings snug in soft babbit
    and washed in pure filtered turbine oil.
I long to press my pulse outward, through miles
    of copper windings.

And the transformer answers—what?
And the disconnects answer—what?
And the boiler master wobbles with the A.G.C.,
And the spray valves answer, diaphragms
    traveling in millimeter precision.

The Dam

Rain now for two days straight.
The floodgates upstream have opened.
Harness and clip in,
dangle the oxygen sensor,
climb
down
narrow
metal
rungs
inside the bascule pier.
Jam a wooden block
inside the hydraulics panel
to stop the piston.

Stride slicker-suited
through downpour
to the north pier
with its siren,
to the gate
with its electric control.

Fumble with the padlock
in the wet and cold.
Open the door,
pull the horn switch over,
three long blasts:

the floodgates upstream have opened,
the water is coming down,
the water is coming.

Hold the stiff red button
firm against the contact.
The winch motor whines
and cable creaks, the gate moans
in complaint as it inches past
faded marks on the pylon,
jerks a bit as the water
rushes under it.

Until the Outage

The beast is all steam breath
and metal intestines. Her attendants climb
the clattering scaffold of stairs
to rope off the heat of leaky refractory.
Recent rains have soaked past lagging
into insulation, and steam hisses up.
The boiler skin bleeds rust.

She isn't young anymore.
Her hydrogen-embrittled boiler tubes
are porous as old bones, cracks spider
from steam drain entries
on the wall of the condenser.
Breakers wear tags like bandages:
burned up bearings, the pump
that just gave up.

She smells of turbine oil
and astringent treated steam.
Her worn bearing seals drip
into bent metal drain troughs, away
from sources of ignition.

The operators coax her along. Last week,
they bypassed #14 Feedwater Heater
when three tubes gave way.
They're gentle with her now,
bring up the pressure slow. *Please*, they ask,
just a little longer. In a few weeks,
the summer will be over.

Turbine Overhaul

All down the turbine floor, the blades arranged
by size like petals of a metal bud
exploded for my view seem delicate
and strange, unfastened from the L. P. hood.
A wobbling fan squeaks out a strain that had
been hushed under the turbine's roaring drone.
Downstairs, two air compressors thump and thud
and hiss. The long, thin blades seem frail and worn.

But I see a foot-long turnbuckle, and tons
stamped on the crane; I watch the struggle one
man has to lever up a blading section's
ten foot bulk. It seems this should go on for months;
the turbine crew has weeks to show their art:
the reassembled elegance of parts.

Lock Out / Tag Out

Remove the power,
place a lock so the contacts
cannot be closed.

Purge the suffocating gas,
dismantle the source.

Bleed off pent-up energy.
Vent the explosive mixture.

Lock them, lock them.
Place a red tag on the lock
and an entry in this book.

Let no one be mistaken
about what is necessary:

I heard of a man, once, dragged
through the narrowest of openings—
the long half-minute death,
the belt they found, streaming
with entrails.

Confined Space Entry

The procedure prepares us,
chant it like a mantra:

one watches at the door;
the entrant precedes with an oxygen monitor.

What to do if he doesn't reply,
the rescuer just as likely to die.

Exhalation

There's nothing like
the smell of searing flesh and fur
to wake from any reverie—
laid across three phases of 480,
bare copper bus bars (the old design),
holes in the floor
of an empty building leading
to this moment

The safety guy, former Marine and EMT,
says burned people smell
that way, too. Hours afterward,
it lingers in the exhalation
as we, the clean-up crew,
long to somehow shed our skin,
empty our pores.

The Lady in White

Downtown, where the old plant slumbered,
the pump room of an older plant remained
with a lone compressor
and two great pipes
that stopped
abruptly outside.

The operator on his daily rounds
unlocked the door,
flicked on his flashlight,
started down the stairs,
was hunting for the wall switch
when he saw her
from the corner
of his eye:
sitting silently on a discharge line,
wearing only white,
smoking a pipe.

They had always wondered
who closed the make-up valves
when none of the operators
could have done it.

Some blamed it on
line vibration, while others
said it was the transients
who slept in corners
of the basement
(though why they would,
no one knew).

That night, the old compressor's
oil went unchecked—the operator
didn't even turn on the light—
left the old pump house
to the lady in white.

The Intimacy of Machines

To stand next to her
as she spins up
feeling the leaking heat
of steam coursing
through blades.

To feel the vibration
as she climbs through the critical,
feel the floating
foundation shake.

To hold the strobe
that steadies the numbers
painted on the whirling shaft.
To watch.

To speak another language:
of blowdown and turning gear
of power relief valves
and impulse blading.

To open the aspirating air.
To insert an oil gun into the furnace.
To latch the trip valve.
To lift a fuel gas safety.

To don flash gear
and pull a breaker.
To enter a confined space.

To burn up a fan.
To accidentally trip the unit.

To stand in the switchyard
when lightning strikes—
a sudden light
a sudden darkness.

To deliberately exercise
the trips.

To rise at 04:30
to begin ministrations at 06:00.
To walk beneath the
dripping cooling water lines
at 23:00 and 03:00.

To seek the source of
oil pooling.
To seek the source
of smoke.

To hunt for the invisible
steam leak
with a rag on a pole.
To hope not
to stand too close.

Glossary

A.G.C.—Automatic Generator Control: an electronic control that directs the generating unit's output with a signal from the electrical dispatch system

Air Preheater—a revolving set of metal baskets that transfers waste heat in the boiler exhaust stack to the boiler's intake air

Aspirating air—air used to counter boiler pressure when opening oil gun ports

Babbitt—a soft metal alloy used for bearings and their housings

Blowdown—a drain valve, often used to remove impurities in boiler water

Commutator and Slip Ring—parts used to transmit electrical energy

Enthalpy—energy in the form of thermodynamic potential

Entropy—a thermodynamic property, related to energetic state

Hood seal—a lead seal that protects the low pressure turbine from overpressure

Knockout tanks—tanks that separate liquid from gas, as in a natural gas line

Ignitor—a spark-actuated pilot light used for igniting gas or oil in the furnace

Impulse and Reaction (Blading)—specialized turbine blades, designed to efficiently transform steam temperature and pressure into kinetic energy

L. P. Hood—the housing for the low pressure section of the turbine

Mollier diagram—a chart describing the enthalpy in a system, including temperatures at which water changes to steam

Preheater—see Air Preheater

Refractory—a material that lines the boiler's furnace, acting as an insulator

Steam gland—a means of sealing the ends of the turbine

Steam table—a table listing the boiling point at water at different pressures

Superheater—section of the boiler in which steam is heated above the saturation point, removing moisture from it so that it behaves as a gas

Turning gear—a gear that turns the turbine shaft when the unit is off-line to keep it from warping

Author's Bio

Cindy Huyser worked at Holly Street Power Plant in Austin, Texas, where she became the first woman to be a Power Plant Control Board Operator and Power Plant Operations Supervisor. She served as co-editor for the 2009 – 2014 editions of the *Texas Poetry Calendar* for Dos Gatos Press, and since 2011 has hosted a monthly poetry reading and open mic at Book Woman in Austin. Her work has appeared in a number of journals and anthologies, including *The Comstock Review, Borderlands: Texas Poetry Review* and Layers (Plain View Press, 1994) in which 20 of her poems are published. She continues to live in Austin, where she now makes her living as a computer programmer.